MARRIED INTO IT

Other books by Patricia Frolander

Grassland Genealogy (Finishing Line Press)

Other volumes in the High Plains Press
POETRY OF THE AMERICAN WEST SERIES

No Roof But Sky, Jane Candia Coleman
Circle of Light, Charles Levendosky
The Red Drum, Jane Candia Coleman
Glass-eyed Paint in the Rain, Laurie Wagner Buyer
Learn to Love the Haze, Robert Roripaugh
Close at Hand, Mary Lou Sanelli
Bitter Creek Junction, Linda M. Hasselstrom
Cloud Seeding, Stacy Gillett Coyle
Beasts in Snow, Jane Elkington Wohl
The White Dove, Jane Candia Coleman
Small Talk, Mary Lou Sanelli

MARRIED INTO IT

Patricia Frolander

Blessings

Patricia Frolander

HIGH PLAINS PRESS

Poetry of the American West Series

Cover art © Sarah Rogers
Used with permission of the artist.
www.sarahrogersart.com

FIRST EDITION

1 3 5 7 9 8 6 4 2

*The Wyoming bucking horse and rider trademark
is federally registered by the State of Wyoming
and is licensed for restricted use through the Secretary of State's office.*

Library of Congress Cataloging-in-Publication Data

Frolander, Patricia.
  Married into it / Patricia Frolander.
    p. cm. -- (Poetry of the American West series)
  ISBN-13: 978-0-931271-96-0
  ISBN-10: 0-931271-96-7 (pbk. : alk. paper)
  1. Ranch life--Wyoming--Poetry. 2. Country life--Wyoming--Poetry.
  3. Wyoming--Poetry. I. Title.
  PS3606.R5845M37 2011
  811'.6--dc22

                                        2011008905

HIGH PLAINS PRESS
403 Cassa Road
Glendo, WY 82213
1-800-552-7819

Catalog available.
www.highplainspress.com

To my husband, Robert,
who always believes in me

⚜CONTENTS

❦PREFACE

In 1969, after seven years of marriage, my husband, Robert, and I left our comfortable home in Denver and headed for his family's cattle ranch in northeastern Wyoming. Our intent was to raise our young children in a rural community where we could spend more time together as a family. We also wanted an environment where our children could learn about nature, husbandry, and responsibility.

Born and reared in cities, I was ill-prepared for the challenges before me. I knew nothing of seventeen-party telephone lines where neighbors listened in on every word, and it had never occurred to me that for five months out of each year I'd make one trip a month to town—for groceries, parts, and whatever ranch supplies might be needed. The idea I might be expected to drive an ailing child to the hospital during a raging blizzard, feeling my way along what might be the road, had never crossed my mind.

I could ride a horse, but aiding cows in birth or feeding motherless lambs was completely beyond my scope. And caring for pigs, chickens, and baby chicks, milking a cow, separating milk, making butter? I don't think so!

Robert had his hands full running the ranch and had no time to mop my tears. Instead, he brought me winter-chilled calves to warm in our bathtub and I mopped up after them. While he was doing the work of three men, I was often on my own—with his patient aunt and two neighbors to occasionally help me learn the basics.

When the children no longer needed my constant supervision, Robert taught me about calving and how to run the machinery. The neighbors watched it all with amusement, enjoying each opportunity for dialogue about my latest *faux pas*. Acceptance into a generational ranching community is difficult. It takes a great deal of time and commitment to become a *bona fide* rancher, but I hope after forty-two years I've earned my spurs.

This lifestyle doesn't suit everyone. The job is physically demanding. Stewardship of natural resources is a must. How hard or how smart you work isn't the deciding factor; it's those unseen forces—weather, disease, markets—that control the outcome, bringing gain or financial ruin. But money in a bank account isn't always a true measure of success and respect.

Often, writing poetry has been my way to get through the hard times, my way to celebrate the freedom and joy of this tough profession. Enjoy these poems I offer in *Married into It,* knowing I give you a brief window into my lifestyle and a sometimes hard look at forty-nine years of partnership between a man and a woman and the ranch they cherish—and hope to pass on to their children.

PATRICIA FROLANDER

MARRIED INTO IT

She'll never last—too much city,
don't know how he stands it.
Imagine! She don't know a heifer from a Hereford.

Oh my, did you hear about her first branding?
Fed them twelve men a four-pound roast
and two burnt apple pies—she'll never make it.

Taught her to milk the cow, did he?
S'pose that's a sight worth seeing;
that old Holstein will kick her plumb to hell.

Those kids of hers, not enough tendin'.
By the way, did you see her garden?
Rows crooked as a dog's hind leg.

I hear she got some chickens.
Bet she turns green dressing them roosters.
She'll need help.

I never! Who ever heard of naming cows and pigs?
Well them pigs rooted up her garden yesterday
and I'll bet she don''t call them by pet names now.

—+— —+— —+— —+— —+—

(continued)

She's had it easy.
He built that house right off, ahead of the machine shed.
Hasn't had to do without like us.

That oldest of theirs is turning out all right,
just like his dad, good breeding.
Those girls will be another story; she'll have her hands full.

I heard she was running the baler.
Now if that don't beat all.
Next thing you know, she'll be running the cows.

He ought to keep her home where she belongs.
She's got no business meddling in menfolk things.
If he hadn't got sick, she'd be tendin' the stove.

Her husband had surgery again,
she and her boy are puttin' up the hay.
I ought to take a hot dish over; she's got her hands full.

—+— —+— —+— —+— —+—

MARRIED INTO IT

Good God, she was over here yesterday
talkin' to my man about semen-testing bulls!
That poor husband of hers—how does he stand it?

She brought a pie to church supper;
s'pose she don't bake too often though.
I'll bet her house is a sight.

Heard she got a computer.
Don't take no machine to run a ranch
just common sense, you gotta be raised with it.

Their fortieth wedding anniversary—
kids are throwin' a party. Guess we'll go.
Good chance to see how the place is holding up.

He and his kin kept that ranch going all these years.
I never! She acts like she owns it or something.
Married into it, she did.   ⱴ

WYOMING

Winds gust history from Cheyenne to Buffalo.
Tales of cattle barons, rustlers, outlaws, homesteaders
are savored with morning coffee,
late-night conversation.

Fort Bridger, Independence Rock, Fort Laramie,
South Pass, Johnson County,
the landscape holds its face—
tacit tales hide in unmarked mounds,
bone-deep scars among bronzed grass.

Chief Washakie, Cattle Kate, John Colter,
Esther Morris, Colonel Nelson Cole—
every town, every trail chronicles
hope, heartbreak, heritage.
People strong in spirit stay,
celebrate miles between settlements.
Sunset riders lope through purpled sage.   ψ

"She'll never last—too much city."

WRINGER WASHER

Rural Wyoming, twelve degrees.

I bucket hot water outside to the washing machine,
more to the rinse tubs, and complain.
Weeks before, in Colorado suburbia, my clothes
washed and dried in automatic appliances.

The bunkhouse I now call home has four rooms
for three children, a dog, and an old wood stove.
Diapers freeze as I pin them to the clothesline.
My mother-in-law predicts:
"You won't last a year."

I grit my teeth and fill another bucket.   ∀

Houston Creek

Houston Creek wends its way
through the heart of the Bear Lodge Mountains,
spills into the Belle Fourche River.
Paint-peeled barns and homesteads nestle generations;
badger, raccoon, gophers, and hawks also call it home.
Along its banks families raise livestock, hay, grain, and gardens.
Chokecherries mingle in draws with bur oak.
Hayfields sprawl in sunshine, wildflowers peep through tall grass.

Secrets live here.

The Rice Ranch cave once kept ice all summer,
cooled lemonade for 1890s picnics in the meadow below.
Coal Mine Hill conceals a whiskey still in a collapsed tunnel,
lures adventurous teens to trouble.

Carved into the side of Rupe Hill is a wagon trace;
when the wind is right you hear the crack of the teamster's whip.
A tornado ripped through the Chatfield ranch, destroyed the barn,
never touched a single shingle on the house sixty feet away.
On the Frolander place, arrowheads surface, testimony to those
who first trailed through ponderosa seeking mulies and white-tails.
On Lambert's land a soddy, its roof caved in, tucks
beside a reservoir—the grave on the north side unmarked.

When snow lies three feet deep, neighbors tell stories over dinner
of wicked horses, rough cattle, tough cowboys.
Grasshoppers, weevil and drought punctuate tales.
Laughter salts each conversation.
Aged eyes mist,
they share secrets with only a few.   ⱽ

BARBED WIRE COMING AND GOING

Seven-buckle overshoes: a requirement,
to open and close five barbed-wire gates,
on the muddy road to civilization.
The '51 Chevy pickup burps,
occasionally squalls like our baby
tucked beside the eight-, five-, and three-year-olds
I take to town once a month.

Unpasteurized milk, cream, butter, and eggs
bring dollars I exchange at the pharmacy
for cough syrup, tablet and pencils, sugar-sweets, new scissors.
The monthly wage dwindles at the grocery
as flour, sugar, coffee, lard, yeast and much more
compete for space in the over-crowded cab.
Bank, post office, parts store, complete my rounds.

Pressed against the cracked window
I bounce from rut to rut
toward our three room
and sort-of-bathroom home.
Spring snowflakes splat the windshield.
Tired wipers strain to clear my view.

Coal stove fired, groceries put away,
peppermint candy soothes
teething daughter, son's stomachache,
and my nerves—
though not enough to cure my aggravation
when I'm asked to make the long drive back to town
to exchange the tractor parts.   ⱱ

18

SECOND TABLE

First neighborhood branding,
the real deal, better than TV westerns!
My contribution to the meal—
chocolate cake.
I will sit among hungry cowboys.

Arriving early at the house
I mention walking to corrals
to watch the roping, the cattle work.
No, my neighbor says,
you'd just be in the way.
Men don't like women in their business.

Coffee burbles,
potatoes steam,
fresh bread awaits the knife,
roast beef braises, brown gravy simmers.
Mouth watering, I can hardly wait.

Cowhands wash,
sit at the extended table,
I prepare to join them.
No, my neighbor says,
second table.
We sit after the men are done,
always been that way. ψ

MOTHERED UP

Meadowlarks and chickadees sing dawn into day.
Frogs and crickets complete the vocal ensemble.
Star-kissed dew shimmers on sheaths of grass,
as whitetail move silently to their bed ground.

My cowboys ride out at first light
to trail our cattle to high country.
Cows call to their calves:
Stay near.
My old mare, left alone in the corral, paces,
tries to catch a glimpse of her companions.

Clouds hide-and-seek the sun.
Wet sheets snap in a newborn breeze.
An apple cake, laced with cinnamon, cools,
while our baby slumbers,
dark silky lashes against pink cheeks.

I know by now the cattle have reached
mountain meadows
where they scent and suckle their young,
A whimper; I nestle and nurse my own,
immersed in her fragrance.

Cotton drapes our bed,
fresh air trapped between warp and weft.
Husband, son, and daughter ride home now
if the drive went as planned.
I snuggle our youngest,

watch a red fox sashay across a draw,
her burrow hidden in a hill not far away.
Soon kits will appear, roll over one another,
nip their siblings and mother in earnest play.
As day draws to a close, my mare nickers:
Welcome home. ⚑

New York to Deadwood

In the hold of his grandma's trunk
bone china rimmed in fourteen carat,
spider-cracked, never used.
Embroidered towels nestle
a yellowed wedding dress,
a tiny bit of lace at collar and cuff
the only ornamentation.
Beneath all, a diary —
fourteen years in a sod house
on Dakota prairie,
living on dust and promises,
while he mined for gold.
Her last entry — in tight, spare script —

"I left the sorry bastard." ⩔

Runaway

I wipe away blood
from a five-inch cut
down my husband's back.

I think about the two-year-old Belgians,
hitched to the hay sled,
running wide-open across the meadows,
snow flying from their hooves,
husband caught under the runners.

Hay bales are scattered for half a mile.
His shredded coat and shirt a reminder
of buried rocks, ice, frozen ground.

I bite my lip as he winces.
Purple bruises appear
on his arms, neck, and chest.

Bandaged,
clean shirt in place,
he stiffly reaches for another jacket,
walks quietly out the door
to unhitch the horses
who dragged him all the way home.   ⱱ

FIRST LABOR

Blond hair escapes her cap.
Coat over her pajamas,
our four-year-old watches,
peers into the lighted shed.

The heifer circles,
seeks a place to lay her swollen body.
Moist air rises
from her distended nostrils.

A small hand holds mine.
My daughter's breath quickens
at first view of birthing,
her blue eyes large with wonder,

The heifer strains in ancient rhythm,
water bursts and tiny hooves appear.
She stands, circles, lies down once more,
stretching, pushing.

Tiny nose follows hooves
thrust forward until the calf lies dark
against the yellow shafts of straw.
He blinks against the light.

An age-old cycle begins:
warm tongue, soft lowing,
the cow urges
her calf to his feet to suckle.

We walk to the house in silence.
Tucked into bed my daughter softly asks,
"Does the baby need a blanket?
I'll give him one of mine."   ψ

"I heard she was running the baler."

JUST ANOTHER DAY AT THE RANCH

A hot and humid hayfield at 5 A.M.,
sneak peek at a blistering day.
I cut hay with an old swather,
open to the elements,
except for the umbrella that dips and sways
with the level of the field.

A gallon water jug, empty by noon,
sits at my feet.
Armies of gnats and bees feed
on my perspiration, deer flies sting,
raise welts and my Irish temper.
Grasshoppers and weevils munch alfalfa,
as I hasten home,
prepare lunch for my family,
and set another gallon of tea in the sun.

Back in the field I struggle to catch breath—
102 degrees at 3 P.M.
Tee shirt soaked, I climb
off the machine to pick up rocks,
replace dull cutting sections.
I fight to stay awake,
a sea of green in front,
rows of hay behind.

I leave the field at dusk,
ponder supper.
Do I really care?
Eleven days down, thirty-four left—
if there are no major breakdowns.

MARRIED INTO IT

Between Fences

The doe hangs lifeless,
one leg tangled in a web of wire,
white flanks exposed.
The eagle begins his work,
flies away when semis spew
snow and slush
into the highway right-of-way.

I quickly look away,
as I have done so often,
from graphic images of other innocents
snared in life's fences.
I focus on the next exit.

FOUR MILES TO THE BELSHE MINE

The story says he chanced it—
hitched the Belgians to the wagon,
slid his way in mud and slush
four miles downhill to the mine.
Loaded anthracite
until springs could hold no more.

The return trip wound upward
then straight up.
Sleet stung his eyes as hooves
the size of dinner plates
sought purchase on the narrow trail.

The wagon sidled,
horses struggled,
their deep combined breaths a dense cloud.
The load slid into scrub oak,
came to a stop,
one wheel butted against a good-sized rock.

MARRIED INTO IT

Winter coats gathered ice
as they rested.
Board-stiff fingers and feet ached.
Over the hill lay home,
family waited.

He popped the geldings hard,
hollered encouragement.
Slowly the wheels began to turn.
He urged them, tears on his cheeks;
those horses had such heart.

Wheels slowed, stopped,
then began to roll backwards.
Horses, coal, wagon, man,
collided in a deep ravine—
wood splintered, horses screamed,
followed by a bone-chilling silence.   ψ

MARRIED INTO IT

Watching the Coyote Dance

He looks skyward,
listens for airplanes dealing death,
trots across the snow-crusted meadow.
His cautious paws zigzag
the fifty-acre pasture.

Abruptly he stops, sits on his haunches,
coarse grey coat lifting in frosty currents.
Head cocks to the right,
ears twitch. He explodes through sunlit air,
pounces on crystallized flakes.

Quarry found, he lopes into a draw,
beds at the opening of his den,
watches the Piper skim the hills
and meadows south of where he lies.
Gold-flecked eyes close in sleep.   ψ

"That oldest of theirs is turning out all right . . .
just like his dad, good breeding."

KINDNESS

Broken posts lean into yesterday's dreams.
Rusty barbed wire rakes autumn wind.
Sunset chases clouds into twilight.

Thin of hair and future, an old stallion
imprints the dusty trail with splayed hooves,
as yesterday's boy saddles a bay,
shoves the rifle into the scabbard,
and rides out.   ⱽ

DENIAL

Our neighbor called it "his ranch,"
yet each winter day found her beside him
feeding hay to hungry cows.

In summer heat,
you would see her in the hayfield,
cutting, raking, baling, stacking.

In between she kept the books,
cooked, cleaned
laundered, fed bum lambs.

Garden rows straight,
canned jars of food
lined cellar walls.

Then she died.
I asked him how he would manage.
"Just like I always have," he said.

REFUGE

High winds shake the lodgepole pine.
Quaking aspen gold lies buried in snow.
Gusts billow our camp tent.
We lie, fingers laced, beneath the quilts
speak softly of decades together.
Embers from the camp stove
flicker against dark shadows,
encourage closer blending.
Secret places found, shared,
invited warmth against the glacial dawn. ⚘

"Those girls of hers will be another story."

IMPRINTING

I wake; it's two in the morning,
time to feed her.

The rains came late this drought year.
The filly came late as well—
too large a foal with legs misshaped,
the color of butterscotch.
The old sorrel mare stood patiently
as I held her offspring to nurse,
a ritual that would continue
every three hours day and night.

Storm brewing, my daughter helps me
move mare and filly to the barn.
We four females define
love between mothers and daughters.

Hoping to straighten, we splint her legs,
warm her with blankets, fall in love
with the nicker that greets each feeding
and the nuzzling she gives so freely.

It was not enough.   ⱽ

THE NOTICE

Down the road
shoulders sag as he leans against the door frame,
gaze following the ridge
as trees become velvet silhouette.

He drinks the scent of freshly cut alfalfa,
a checkerboard of bales fading from hollow view.

Bile rising,
he wipes the moisture from his hatband
with a word that frames his life's work —foreclosure.

COMMITMENT

Six inches of snow churned into mud
as the cow circles the stiffening body,
lowing,
urging her calf to rise.

Five days she guards his lifeless form,
from coyotes
and me,
as I leave a daily ration of hay.   ⱱ

GOOSE DOWN

Canada geese fly south
bear summer on wings,
honk warnings to sparrows
who linger in cedars and pines.
Mice burrow in haystacks and barns
as the month of Sagittarius approaches.
Elk boast heavy hair, their bugles
carried away in October wind.

What of my winter warmth?
After months of drought
I pray for a goose down coat
and heavy blankets of snow.

OLD RELIABLE

The truck is sooty black,
rusted tailpipe and fenders faded
to gun-metal gray,
her sunken seat worn comfortable with the years.

I used to turn that pickup loose
after putting her in granny gear,
jump out the door and vault onto the flatbed
stacked with small square bales.

Every now and then she'd jerk,
a tire slipping over a frozen cow pie,
then lurch in a new direction
as I struggled for balance.
A meandering trail of hay traced
over crusted snow and small drifts
shadowed blue-gray on overcast days.

In the biggest meadow,
it took time to feed those bawling cows—
kept an eye on where I was 'cause
the west side draw was pretty deep.
My husband wouldn't understand
if I was to roll the old girl,
she's all we had to drive
and I never liked to walk in hard-shelled snow.

Now a John Deere tractor takes her place.
A large round bale peels off the spear
like lemon from its rind.
"Makes the work easier," he says,
"no worry about where you're going."
He says, "Just drive," so I do.   ∜

Between the West Pasture and Home

The saddlebags are dusty,
hung over a wooden rail
that separates the tack room
from the stalls.
In nineteen years the leather
has dried and cracked,
but the bloodstains are visible
if you know where to look.

Her brother tooled the leather,
grinned when he handed them to their dad
who mumbled something about fancy
but the bags decorated the back of his saddle
every year thereafter—fit staples,
fencing pliers, a small roll of wire,
canteen, chew, Bag Balm, and binoculars.
Hardly ever room for a sack lunch,
but he could wedge an apple
for the small daughter
who rode beside him on an old mare.

MARRIED INTO IT

He was fencing on the hogback ridge,
between the west pasture and home,
when the bullet hit him square
in the back of his head.
Didn't suffer, friends said, that was good.
Some damned hunter
with a high-powered rifle, quick trigger,
and buck fever.
So they said.

I don't know who put his gear away,
turned out his horse. I do know
the man who married their mama the next year
was a damn good shot.   ⱴ

"He ought to keep her home where she belongs."

ATTITUDE

Breeze stirs barely-grayed hair
his heart set on walleye supper
eyes intent on the pole

heart set on living each day
against the odds
the doctor gave after
the third open heart —
ten bypasses
two stents
seventeen angioplasties
anaphylactic shock
serum sickness
all in nineteen years

heart set on another tomorrow   Ⅴ

OVERSIGHT

I need a man to fence,
dig holes, plant posts,
stretch barbed wire.

He wears a sweat-stained Stetson.
Tired gray eyes
match his frayed shirt.
Sinewy, soft-spoken,
a man of little education.
Whiskey breath and weather-cracked lips
tell his story.

Don't need your help, he says.

Each week I ride out,
see how he is doing.
My fourth trip,
says he'll be on his way—
doesn't like working for a nosy woman.

TEMPEST

She sits amid native grass on a high ridge
embraced by pine, cedar, and oak.
Miles away a storm
spills down the Big Horn Mountains,
races onto the Wyoming plains
like a thousand chariots whose driving winds
chill through her heavy coat.

She should seek shelter,
yet the panorama holds her fast.
The trees draw in a long deep breath,
brace themselves for the oncoming snow.
Nearby aspen rattle as clouds
scuttle over the undulating landscape.
A prairie falcon searches for a roost.

She rises to her feet, startles a squirrel,
whose scolding voice pierces the gray afternoon.
The does who were feeding on the meadows
now hasten into draws once lined with chokecherry leaves.
She wonders how long it will be
before he finds she's gone.

FRESH PASTURE

In the timber, flies and ticks
wait to feast on tender flesh.
Bulls brush up, heat riding their backs.

Horse sweat, dust, and I
meet a moss-covered spring.
My bandanna swipes away green algae.

I bend into cool water,
drink deeply
of fulfillment met in solitary places.   ⱱ

HIRED HAND

He sprawls against his saddle
in a weathered red barn.
Whiskey snores drift
into the corral
where three horses stiffen
in churned dirt and manure—
sorrel and bay hides sweat-dried
eyes rolled back,
velvet muzzles covered in dirt.

He left the granary door open.
Poisoned oats spilled across the floor,
down the steps.

Horses: 3
Rats: 0   ⅋

GRASSLAND GENEALOGY

Prairie seeds, dirt and thistle
borne on biting wind,
adorn wooden crosses,
mausoleums, marble stones,
and the small chapel steps.

This last refuge, draped over a hill
bears its earthy blanket with dignity.
Tears more frequent than rain
nurture native roots, their grasp
as tenacious as the pioneers they embrace.

I greet the ancient ones.
Spirits move with the breeze,
hover beyond my shoulder
wondering why I am here.
I whisper my answer to the November sunset. ▼

480 SECONDS

The hayfield is an oven, humid for Wyoming.
All afternoon low-hanging clouds obscure the horizon.
Rhythm of baler, drone of tractor
lull my senses, lure me to slumber.

Suddenly, sixth sense uneasiness,

I watch a dark green cloud on the move.
Fourth gear, I head for home.

Horses race down the ridge into pine trees.
Cows bawl for unseen calves.
Our dog howls as I park the tractor,
yell to our children
as the first icy pellets hit my back.

Children, dog, and I meet at the back door,
hurry to close windows and curtains.
Staccato hail deafens,
windows explode in shards of glass.

Eight minutes of terror.

I open the door to a moonscape.
Fields of hay are flattened,
ripened acres of grain, crushed.
Two-thirds of our income gone
in 480 seconds.

MARRIED INTO IT

CHICKADEE

Bent to his task,
he's snug in gray downy coat with white muffler,
tail feathers tipped with each gust of hurrying wind.
He forages the last seeds of summer
under snow-laden blue spruce.
Does he remember sunny breakfasts,
the weight of early harvests
making it difficult to fly?

THREE GRAVES BY THE RIVER

Barren branches pierce low-hanging clouds.
Scattered picket fencing
abandons leaning headstones
etched with names

        Colter
Mary and Baby Elizabeth
        1907

        Colter
        Thomas
        1907

        Colter
        Martin
        1907

Dried leaves scuttle, crackle like old bones
their colors bled in autumn winds.   ψ

MARRIED INTO IT

BANDAGING LOVE

The bay mare stands patiently, almost asleep,
as I soothe her aching muscles with sharp-smelling liniment.

Years ago, she was our best cutting horse.
          She will finish her days here—
tall grass in summer, hay and warm shelter in winter.
Love and silent conversation seal our relationship.

I can't mend the mare's legs
any more than I can mend
my children's crippled hearts.
I bury my face against the mare's neck.
My dearest friend listens,
          soothing me as only she can.   Ⱶ

HOSTAGE

They hide among green leaves.
Drenched with dew, suspended,
the dark red delight promises jam or jelly,
a gentle slide down a slope of sherbet,
or marriage to shortcake and heavy cream.

Raspberries hold me hostage.
With crimson lips I plead my guilt.
I am a willing prisoner.   ∜

"She's had it easy."

SPRING TRAINING

Fencing time.
Back, legs and arms quiver
as the post driver vibrates through my body.
Muscles contract as I pull
fence stretchers,
splice wires parted by winter snows.
A two-gallon sprayer seems light at first,
as I climb hills, spray weeds.
Sweat bees lunch on my exertion.

Muscle cramps
jump me out of bed,
throbbing reminders of aging limbs.
Checking cows and calves,
my saddle horse and I regret the weight
winter naps have settled.
Sunburned cheeks and shoulders
tan with each day's labor;
pick rock, till soil, plant seed.

No fitness trainer, gym, or track
define my daily workouts.
Ranching is my spring training ground.

SISTERHOOD

Tonight I finished reading your book.
Before the Dream Gatherer claims me,
I ride east across the Black Hills,
ask forgiveness for intruding on your solitude.
My calloused hands reach for yours in greeting;
in quiet voices we speak of calving and moisture.

Like prairie grass that bows before the wind,
we share life—so many parallels.
Urban education
prepared us to claim the land with tears of relief,
privilege of good horses, strong calves, full reservoirs
and the love of a man who fits the missing pieces of our souls.

With wind-chapped cheeks and wrinkle lines
proclaiming seasons in the sun,
we laugh at the jokes life has played on us,
frown at those who would rearrange our lives.

Those who are not challenged by the seasons,
the need to give back a portion of what they have used,
to give value to hard work, bring honor to friendship,
cannot understand our need for extremes in life.

As dawn breaks, I warm the bit in my hands
before I slip it into the buckskin's mouth.
With tightened cinch I lead her into the chill air
and turn . . .

The cold air slips beneath my blankets.
I waken wondering if you saw me wave goodbye.   ∀

SEASONS

That was me dancing in the wildflowers,
damp with dew and love,
twirling to passion's music—
laughing, luminous.

That was me in the hayfield
heavy with heat and desire to please,
blushing with pleasure, blood rushing
like drumbeats. Oh yes,
and in the mountain tent,
bared skin soft as snowfall,
canvas refuge moaning in winds
of the canyons.

And that was me weeping among faded blooms
and broken stems of wheatgrass,
the melody drained,
only echoes in deserted soil.   ⸙

Neighborhood Watch

Coiffed salt and pepper,
silver grey, a blonde with brown roots,
sit at the local café table for eight,
discuss the rain, lousy coffee,
and Edna Mae's cancer treatment.
Doughnut and English muffin crumbs
witness Nelson's divorce settlement,
the Taylor boy's DWI,
this year's might-be-pregnant prom queen.
The siren breaks their concentration,
chairs screech as the three hasten to the window.
Gathering umbrellas, coats and plastic scarves
they pay their checks,
promise to call, as soon as they know
who's sick or died.   ∳

WHY I STAY

for awakening grass and chokecherry leaf,
a flute-warbled song from a yellow throat,
a heart, quickened, at springtime blush.
I revel in rain-drenched fields,
ramble meadows and hillsides,
seek coyote and fox,
glimpse fawns nestling in tall grasses.

I rouse to calls of Canada geese,
their vee slicing blue air,
seek the bandit who eats my winter grain,
laugh at ducklings' play in the reservoir,
rejoice at the stallion's nicker calling his mares.
I stay for the rhythm of season,
for the land, always the land,
and
for a man whose hands know my heartbeat
almost as well as God knows my soul. ⱱ

EZRA

The first volley of shots
slams against our ears,
pierces our hearts,
takes away our breath.

Afternoon sunshine rests
on the flag-draped coffin
that will soon reside
with his fallen comrades.

He cheated death on the battlefield
but disease riddled his eighty-three-year-old body.
A lingering death—
bullets would have been kinder.

He reached out
through a morphine haze,
work-worn hands a plea
for help, kindness, love.

Those same hands held a rifle,
fashioned homes,
cradled our children,
crafted our friendship.

He wanted to come home
to die in the house he'd built
and the arms of a family
who claimed him—

and he did.

BOYS DON'T CRY

He holds the phone to his chest.
Ten-year-old shoulders
shake silently.
I give him time to collect his pride.

"Gosh, I hate to see you leave so soon,"
I say with a catch in my throat.
"Gee Gram, I don't have to go.
Dad has stuff to do again."
"Well, let's go check the heifers."
He nods assent, forces a smile,
hangs up the phone.

Where do unfinished tears fall
when a man tells his son
"Boys don't cry."   ⅋

JOHNNY VAN

Handsome, broad-chested, well-muscled,
with bad habits I thought I could change.
I was wrong. Too many years of getting his way,
spoiled him rotten.
I knew from the beginning I was in for a hell of a ride.

I anticipated, maneuvered,
was always caught off-guard—
always hurt.

My age was the deciding factor.
After six years of heartache and multiple bruises,
I let him go
to a young cowgirl with a hard edge
and a penchant for a first-class roping horse.   ⚘

Bit by Bit

She's been leaving his place for years—
Like a bird, rising with hope,
finds her wings clipped.

He's fed her just enough fear;
sullied her,
shredded her.

Caged in an old ranch house,
severed from family and friends,
she searches for salvation.

Today, wind blows bitter through prairie landscape.
She flies on, feathers scattered behind.   ψ

ON A BITTER DAY

translucent membranes wrap
a lifetime of memories.
Firm jaw gone slack,
mouth open in winter sleep,
cold callused hands rest
their weary flesh.
Goodbyes past hearing,
heartbeat stilled,
in a room too small for grief. ∀

Army of Innocents

They pose by the kitchen table.
The oldest holds his arms wrapped around
an invisible rifle,
our second aims directly at the lens,
while our granddaughter blows smoke from her finger barrel.
The four-year-old smiles, holds his toy pistols high,
I shudder at the click of the camera.   ∀

"I never! She acts like she owns it or something."

LONG-TERM EDUCATION

spring blizzards
hot-as-hell summers, sweat bees in my shirt
machinery determined to break down
backward calves, prolapsed cows
six-hundred-pound weaning weights
three good stock dogs when we half hoped
for just one dandy

children's heartaches
patched jeans
champion steer at the livestock fair
tears of anguish when he sold
smoke-filled lungs from branding fires
wind-tangled hair
chokecherry picking

biting wind and heavy snow
sleds of hay for livestock
fencing
always fencing
years of age sag the wires
and my belly
forty years, no ranching diploma—
just passed my freshman year

TO AFRICA

I nestle into the shoulder of the chair,
legs draped over the side,
laundry abandoned,
dishes lying in cold, soapy water.

Soon I am lost in creamy pages,
jostled with each camel-step
as I follow a white-robed Bedouin
through heat-heavy sand.

Four pages later I glide
onto Nairobi airport tarmac.
Scarlet bougainville hides the shards of glass
in concrete walls that guard elite homes.

The Rift Valley lies in the next chapter.
A pride of lions attack a Grevy's zebra.
Hardly able to breathe, I turn the page,
am startled by an inquiring ostrich.

I skirt the Maasai cattle near the Serengeti,
turn east towards Mombasa.
Tourist pleasures await
the heroine and me.

Hours later I stiffly rise
when my arriving spouse
asks where I went today?
Amused, I tell him glibly,
to Africa.

LIFE FLIGHT

I meet Death at the usual crossroads,
his face shadowed by the hood
of his cape.

Our eyes engage, my courage
slips away in the moonlight,
fear heavy in my bones.

He nods, turns into the silence.
I hear a siren
and struggle for breath.   Ⱶ

"She's got no business doing that . . . and at her age."

RED HAT SOCIETY

I age into a baggy purple shirt
worn with a red sweater as homely
as ancient cable knit can get.
No amount of promised skin renewal
can fill the creviced cheeks.
I look for the girl who lives within.

Reflections of youth are bittersweet.
Sixteen, I struggled for composure.
Sixty-eight, I struggle for balance of mind and body.
Like a hummingbird sipping nectar,
I hurry through each day
tasting precious moments.

I cast aside convention,
travel barefoot into the garden
in moonlight, in a sheer nightgown,
to taste ripe tomatoes.
I sit down beside the scarecrow wearing
the cast-off purple shirt.
I'll keep the sweater.

INSOMNIA

Late night minutes
pile around my knees,
anchor me to the writing chair.
Sleepy thoughts ebb and flow
as black letters spill on white paper,
hours stolen from rhythm of dreams.
Scattered are ribbons of thoughts
and chocolate chip cookie crumbs.   ⑃

SENTINEL

Ground shudders,
limbs snap, as ponderosa
meets earth.
Chainsaw silenced; quiet envelops me.
I kneel,
count her rings;
one hundred twenty-two inside riddled bark.

While the pine was a sprout,
long before bark beetle found this home,
great-granddad cleared ranch fields
of petrified wood, igneous rock,
sandstone inlaid with belemnites.

When the ponderosa was a sapling,
Wyoming became a state.
Grandma was born when
this tree was twenty summers strong.
In evergreen maturity,
buried in snow halfway up her trunk,
she survived the Winter of '49.

MARRIED INTO IT

Needles died
as I cradled my great-grandchild.
Bark no longer protected her core,
she stood one last winter,
dignity ravaged.

Her fire blazes
October through April,
warms our home and hearts.
Where she once stood,
a sapling greets coming generations.   🌱

GENESIS

You are my Adam, made of gumbo, rock, and wind.
Scarred, bold hands confirm your labor,
back slightly bent, you lean into the land.
Shadowed canyons crevice your cheeks,
worry and laugh lines corner your eyes.
Illness lingers.
Shorter steps, shorter breath, but enough
to reach my arms.
I am your Eve, your rib, your thorn,
and always your love. ⱱ

Approaching Hibernation

Overnight the world is etched.
Frost-edged stems of grass
marry icy flowers.
Trees reach into glacial sky.

Geese break the trail
as fall rides winter's winds
scattering leaves
of buckskin, umber, scarlet.

Apparitions graze
in fog-kissed meadows,
and marrow burrows
deep into cooling earth. ∜

GRASS-HELD DREAMS

I follow old wagon tracks,
thistle here and there among the grasses.
The freight trail winds up
among scrub oak heavily hung in green shade.
I carefully pace my memories.

Over the next rise,
a tryst in golden leaves.
Around the bend a cranky bull wouldn't move
out of the bur oak thicket.
To my right an old fox den hid five kits.

Out of breath, I watch a porcupine
peer between ponderosa needles,
cambium crumbs on his chin.

I clamor to the ridge top
where breath meets sky.
Cedar and pine spill down the hillsides
to droughty meadows, empty stock ponds,
and cattle long gone.

Tomorrow, we'll sign over the deed—
half the ranch
gone. ⱽ

PREDATORS

Homesteaders moved to the plains,
Black Hills, Omaha, Cheyenne,
Klamath Falls—
    settled the country,
developed water, built roads,
toughed out blizzards and drought,
survived,
blistered hands and dirty fingernails
testimony.
They saved money, paid with cash,
    doing without was no shame.

Now the silhouette of government
looms on the horizon,
dictates wildlife species
are more important than people.
Well-meaning citizens give to
feel-good organizations,
tie ranchers in litigation,
force them out of business,
then sell the land they "saved."
Who then, nurtures the land and wildlife?

Winds of change blow.
It's hard to recognize
the wolves.   ψ

"She'll never last; too much city."

FATHER WHEN YOU CALL

let me be feeding horses in the big pasture
at five below zero
inhaling scent of alfalfa, breath frosting eyelashes
years written on my face
not in my heart

or let me be fencing in the west pasture
pulling up wire from pungent earth
where snow bent its back
tightening each strand against errant calf
while meadowlarks greet springtime's blush

or let me be gathering in the hills
content to drink from a battered canteen
the sweetest water in Crook County
the Heeler quick to roust a cow from brush
my mare eager to turn a stray

or let me be sleeping in the old ranch house
next to my partner
whose gentle snores match my own
arthritic hands joined
horse-miles and hay-miles behind us   ¥

MARRIED INTO IT

⚡ ᴀCKNOWLEDGMENTS

I want to express my deepest gratitude to Bearlodge Writers. These gifted individuals have strengthened my work with their suggestions and editing, but most importantly, they have given me encouragement and support as I refined each poem. My life is blessed and enriched by their friendships.

Noted Black Hill artist Sarah Rogers generously allowed me to use her painting, *Caballos Pintados,* on the cover of the book. I am honored and thrilled to share her work with readers.

—+— —+— —+— —+— —+—

"Wringer Washer," *Poets of the American West,* Many Voices Press, 2010.

"New York to Deadwood," *Poets of the American West,* Many Voices Press, 2010.

"Denial," *American Life in Poetry* (Column 275) compiled by Ted Kooser, U.S. Poet Laureate, 2004-2006. *American Life in Poetry* is made possible by The Poetry Foundation, publisher of *Poetry* magazine. It is also supported by the Department of English at the University of Nebraska–Lincoln.

"Imprinting," won second place in the WyoPoets National Contest through the National Federation of State Poetry Societies, 2004.

"Long Term Education," *Hard Ground IV: Writing the Rockies,* Pronghorn Press, 2003.

"Approaching Hibernation," *Owen Wister Review,* 2007.

"Father When You Call," winner of the Seventeenth Annual National Senior Poets Laureate Competition (2009), sponsored by Amy Kitchner's Angels Without Wings Foundation.

❦ THE ᴀUTHOR

Patricia Frolander tries to balance family, ranching, and writing and has a passion for each of them. In 1985 she and her husband, Robert, purchased the ranch his great-grandfather homesteaded in 1885, in the Black Hills of Wyoming. Their family includes three children, seven grandchildren, and two great-grandchildren, all of whom live close to the ranch. You may find her on a tractor or horse, but at this stage of her life she prefers the padded office chair at her writing desk.

Patricia's first book, *Grassland Genealogy,* was published in 2009. Her poetry has been widely published in numerous anthologies, included in American Life in Poetry (Column 275) by Ted Kooser, former U.S. Poet Laureate. She was the recipient of the 2011 Neltje Blanchan Award through the Wyoming Arts Council, the winner of the 17th Annual National Senior Poets Laureate Competition sponsored by Amy Kitchner's Angels Without Wings Foundation (2009); Guest Poet at the Matthews Opera House feature, *Stars Shine 2008;* Featured Poet at the 2007 Alzada Cowboy Poetry, Music and Art Show; and has been featured in journals, magazines and newspapers.

The text is eleven-point Berkeley Oldstyle Book
by the International Type Company.
Display type is Confection and Understudy by Letterhead Fonts.
The ornaments are We Love Nature Leaves by Kapitza
and LHF Engraver's Ornaments.
The book is printed on
fifty-five pound Nature's Natural
(a fifty-percent post-consumer recycled paper, processed acid free)
by Thomson-Shore.

green press
INITIATIVE

High Plains Press is committed to preserving ancient forests
and natural resources. We elected to print this title on 30%
postconsumer recycled paper, processed chlorine-free. As a
result, for this printing, we have saved:

2 Trees (40' tall and 6-8" diameter)
789 Gallons of Wastewater
1 million BTUs of Total Energy
50 Pounds of Solid Waste
175 Pounds of Greenhouse Gases

High Plains Press made this paper choice because our printer,
Thomson-Shore, Inc., is a member of Green Press Initiative,
a nonprofit program dedicated to supporting authors, publish-
ers, and suppliers in their efforts to reduce their use of fiber
obtained from endangered forests.

For more information, visit www.greenpressinitiative.org

Environmental impact estimates were made using the Environmental Defense
Paper Calculator. For more information visit: www.edf.org/papercalculator